NORAGAMI
STRAY GOD
ADACHITOKA
EPi

characters

YATO

A minor deity who always wears a sweatsuit.

YUKINÉ

Yato's shinki who turns into swords.

HIYORI IKI

A high school student who has become half ayakashi.

KOFUKU

A goddess of poverty who calls herself Ebisu, after the god of fortune.

DAIKOKU

Kofuku's shinki who summons storms.

EBISU

A business-god in the making, one of the Seven Gods of Fortune.

KUNIMI

A shinki who enhances Ebisu's motor skills.

NANA

A powerful shinki who once rebelled against the Heavens.

BISHAMONTEN

A powerful warrior god, one of the Seven Gods of Fortune.

KAZUMA

A navigational shinki who serves as guide to Bishamon.

TAKEMIKAZUCHI

A warrior god who longs for the chaos of war.

KIUN

Takemikazuchi's shinki who has earned the title of Thunder Blade.

KÔTO FUJISAKI

Yato's "father."

STRAY

A shinki who serves an unspecified number of deities.

A WELCOME SURPRISE!
I HAD HOPED FOR A WEAPON.
AND YOU GIVE ME GARB AS WELL. YOU ARE A MULTI-PURPOSE SHINKI!
STILL...

AY!
FIDGET FIDGET
...IT IS SOMEWHAT SINISTER. I LOOK QUITE THE VILLAIN IN THIS ATTIRE.
...ALTHOUGH... IN A SENSE, I SUPPOSE I AM.
HE WOULD NEVER APPROVE OF THESE METHODS.
FORGIVE ME, KAZUMA.

CHAPTER 60: WHAT THE HEAVENS BRING ABOUT

KAZUMA-SAN!
WHAT'S THE MATTER?
WHERE IS OJÔ?
OH, I, UH, JUST CAME TO GET SOME-THING...
I'LL BE GOING BACK TO THE DIVINE COUNCIL, AND I'LL BE OUT FOR A WHILE... KURAHA, LOOK AFTER THE OTHERS.

...IS THAT REALLY WHERE YOU'RE GOING?
WHAT?
SPARE ME THE INNOCENT ROUTINE. YOU'RE WHITE AS A SHEET.
YOU AND OJÔ BOTH NEED TO STOP KEEPING EVERYTHING TO YOUR-SELVES.
AND TELL US WHAT'S GOING ON.
WE NEED TO BE UNITED.
WE'RE ALL HERE TO HELP.

...I'M SORRY.
BISHAMON-SAMA HAS DISAPPEARED.

...WHAT? BUT I THOUGHT ANÉ-SAMA WAS AT THE DIVINE COUNCIL.
SHE'S NOT?! THEN WHERE...?
I SUSPECT...
...SHE WENT TO NAKATSU-KUNI TO GET THE SEALED BLESSED VESSEL...
WHY WOULD SHE DO THAT?! SHE HAS A BLESSED VESSEL, KAZUMA-SAN—YOU!
GRR?!

BISHAMON-SAMA IS GOING TO CONFRONT HIM.
THE CRAFTER.
...TO AVENGE TSUGUHA?! ALONE?!
YEAH! WHY DIDN'T SHE COME TO US?!
MY THEORY IS THAT WHAT-EVER IT WAS THAT TURNED TSUGUHA INTO AN AYAKASHI CAME FROM THE CRAFTER.
THEN I HAVE TO FIGHT WITH HER!!
IT HAD TO!! TSUGUHA WOULD NEVER HAVE STUNG ANÉ-SAMA!!
...THAT'S WHY.
THAT'S WHY SHE LEFT US BEHIND.

THERE'S STILL SO MUCH WE DON'T KNOW ABOUT THE CRAFTER AND HIS ABILITIES... IT'S FOOLISHNESS TO GO AFTER HIM ALONE.
THIS IS HER WAY OF KEEPING ALL OF US OUT OF DANGER.
BUT... SHE DIDN'T EVEN WANT ME.
TMP
WH-WHOA?!
CRNK
KURA-HA...
PULL YOURSELF TOGETHER, KAZUMA-SAN! THIS IS NO TIME TO BE MOPING!
I'LL BE YOUR LEGS! TELL ME WHERE TO GO!

...!
I'M SORRY. ...THANK YOU!
SHE'S WORKING IN SECRET FOR A REASON! DON'T LET THE OTHERS KNOW ABOUT IT...AND DON'T LET THE HEAVENS FIND OUT, EITHER!
KINUHA, I'M LEAVING YOU IN CHARGE!
OKAY!
GRR!
LET'S GO! KURAHA!
WE'RE GOING TO STOP VEENA!

RATTLE...
FIRST ONE HERE!
I HAVE BEEN RIDING MY BIKE TO SCHOOL SINCE WE MOVED. MAYBE I'M GETTING STRONGER.
GOOD FOR ME!
CLUNK
EH HEH. I BROUGHT IT TO SCHOOL.

IT'S BEEN THREE DAYS DOWN HERE, BUT YATO AND YUKINÉ-KUN ARE STILL AT THE DIVINE COUNCIL... I HOPE THEY COME BACK SOON.
WOW... IT'S BEEN A YEAR SINCE I MET EVERYONE.
WE HAD AN EARLY SNOW THAT DAY... I WONDER IF THAT'S WHY YATO NAMED HIM YUKINÉ?
THE NAME ANSWERS, THE VESSEL TO SOUND.
WAIT. DOES THAT MEAN YUKINÉ-KUN IS ONE YEAR OLD?
THE NAME, YUKI.
THE VESSEL, SETSU.
IT WOULD BE NICE TO CELEBRATE HIS BIRTH-DAY...

...
YATOGAMI-SAMA... I PRAY THAT WE CAN ALL BE FRIENDS AGAIN...AND HAVE FUN TOGETHER LIKE WE USED TO!
CLAP CLAP

ZSHH

WAAAAHH!!
MY EYES ARE BURNING!!
YOUR EYES WILL ADJUST SOON ENOUGH. HAVE PATIENCE SHIKKI.
GYAAAAH!!
YOU LITTLE... DON'T ACT LIKE YOU'RE THE BOSS OF ME!
I HAVEN'T...
...BOWED TO THE HEAVENS...
...YET...

WHAT... WHAT IS THIS?
A VIL-LAGE?
... OUS-ES?

THERE ARE SO MANY PEOPLE.
ゴオッ
WHOOSH
GYAAAAAH!!!
ぎゅるんっ
GWHRR
MRK!

WHAT WAS THAT?! THERE WERE PEOPLE IN ITS BELLY!!
KA-CLUNK
KA-CLUNK...
THAT IS WHAT THEY CALL A TRAIN. PEOPLE RIDE IT FROM PLACE TO PLACE.
...I SEE YOUR EYES HAVE ADJUSTED.
!
JOLT
FWOOSH
THE WORLD OF MEN HAS CHANGED DRASTICALLY SINCE YOU WERE SEALED AWAY.
WHAT THINK YOU OF TODAY'S WORLD?
HAS IT IN ANY WAY APPROACHED THE WORLD FOR WHICH YOU HOPED?
...NGH...

NO, SHUT UP! THE HEAVENS ARE NOTHING BUT EVIL!!
YOU PEO-PLE—
GRUMBLE
GURGLE GURGLE
GRUMBLE...
YOU ARE A NOISY ONE, AREN'T YOU?
WELL... THEY SAY AN ARMY MARCHES ON ITS STOMACH
RETURN AWHILE, NANA.
KHEEN
WAIT HERE.

BAM

CRISP...

...DID YOU PEOPLE DO THIS, TOO?
HOW CAN YOU THINK THAT? THE HEAVENS MERELY GIVE.
ONLY HUMANS CAN CULTIVATE.
RUSTLE RUSTLE
THIS RICE IS FROM THE NEW HARVEST. GO ON, EAT.
INCH INCH

SNATCH
CHOMP CHOMP CHOMP
MGH! COUGH COUGH!!
THIS WON'T DO...I FEEL MYSELF GROWING FOND OF HER. BUT I HAVE NO INTENTION OF GIVING HER A HA NAME.

SO AT THE VERY LEAST...
...I SHAN'T LET HER DIE ALONE.

WHOOSH
NOW TO PUT YOU TO WORK.
BRING THE MAN KNOWN AS THE CRAFTER INTO THE OPEN AND KILL HIM.
IF ALL GOES WELL, I SHALL GIVE YOU THE HEAVENS' HEAD AND A PLACE TO DIE.
...HMPH.
SO YOU ARE WITH THE HEAVENS.

SOMETIMES, THE HEAVENS TAKE TOO MUCH.
FZHH
FWA-WHOOSH

KA-CRASH
?!
SHATTER
CLATTER
ガランガラン
CLATTER
WHAT ...?
AAAAAHH!
CRASH
ガシャーン
WHAT HAPPENED?!
I'M SCARED!
W-WAS T THE VIND?
DID OME-HING EX-ODE?!
ビュオオオオ
WHOOSH

THE OTHER CLASS-ROOMS ARE IN BA SHAPE, TOO...
IT'S NOT SAFE BY THE WINDOW! COME INSIDE!!
SOME-ONE'S THERE... A WOMAN?
THA HAIR.
IT CAN'T BE... BISHA-MON-SAN?!
SMIRK

BUT EVERY-ONE'S LOOKING FOR HER! WHAT IS SHE DOING HERE?!
DON'T TELL ME SHE'S REALLY GOING TO FIGHT FUJI-SAKI-SEM-PAI!

BA-BOOM
...WHAT WAS THAT?
IT LOOKED LIKE BISHAMON... DID KAZUMA TELL HER WHERE TO FIND ME?

WELL, HE WHO FIGHTS AND RUNS AWAY...
BUT DID SHE ALWAYS HAVE A SHINKI LIKE THAT?
KER-SPLASH
YOU CAN SEE ME.
THMP
URK ...?!

WHEN I LOOKED OVER THE SCHOOL, MY EYES MET THOSE OF HIYORI IKI...
...AND YOURS.
...YOU TAKE THE FORM OF A MORTAL.
WHY DO YOU RAVAGE HEAVEN AND EARTH?
CRAFTER.

FOR FUNSIES.
I'VE LIVED A LONG TIME, BELIEVE IT OR NOT. AND LIFE IS AWFULLY DULL IF YOU HAVE NO WAY TO ENJOY IT.
YOU THINK THAT FUN? YOU...
YOU WILL PAY FOR ...
I'LL PAY? REALLY.
ECAUSE, S USUAL, YOU'RE O MUCH BETTER HAN ME.
YOU, THE LIKES OF A GOD.

YOUR ILK GET OFF SCOT-FREE FOR EVERY-THING YOU DO.
BUT WHO DO YOU THINK FORGIVES THE DEBT?
PEOPLE DO.
NO MATTER HOW MUCH YOU TAKE FROM THEM HOW MUCH YOU WALK ALL OVER THEM.
THEY JUST ACCEPT IT WITHOUT A WORD OF COMPLAINT.
I CAN'T FORGIVE ANY OF YOU.
NOT THE GODS...OR ANY OF THE IDIOTS WHO FORGIVE THEM.

THEY'RE LIKE LITTLE CHILDREN WHO DO NOTHING BUT CRY AND CLING TO THEIR PARENTS...
...NO MATTER HOW MUCH OF A BEATING THOSE PARENTS GIVE THEM.
YOU SAY THIS IS THE WORLD THAT MEN AND GODS ALL WANTED...
AND THAT MAKES ME...
...WANT TO SHAKE THINGS UP!

...YOU ARE A CHATTY ONE.
I KNOW, RIGHT? I THINK I'M JUST EXCITED THAT I GET TO BE MYSELF FOR A CHANGE.
YOU'RE LOOKING GOOD, TOO, BISHAMON. LIKE A SUPER VILLAIN.
...YES, I THOUGHT SO, TOO.
HA! SO YOU ADMIT IT.
COME!
CHIKI ...

FWOOSH
?!
FWISH
THUNK
THUNK
THUNK
THUNK
THUNK

CLATTER
...WHAT.. IS THIS?
CLATTER
CLATTER
NO! IT IS TOO SOON!
HERE THEY COME...
THE HEAVENS!
BOOM
BOOM

BOOM
BOOM
BOOM

A-ALL OF YOU! LIS-TEN!
BOOM
THE CRAFTER— THE SOURCE OF CALAMITY! HE IS HERE BEFORE—
RRRAAAHH
TAKE-MIKA-ZUCHI ...

RRRRAAAAH
...WHEW, WHAT A RELIEF.
THE HEAVENS ARE ON MY SIDE!
CHAPTER 60 / END

神

SO VEENA HAS BEEN HERE...
SHOULD WE SPLIT UP AND LOOK FOR HER, KAZUMA-SAN?
YES, LET'S DO THAT.
TMP
THE BURIER...
THE ONE WHO TORE HEAVEN AND EARTH ASUNDER... WAS SEALED... IN THIS?
COULD VEENA REALLY BREAK THE SEAL WITHOUT ANY CONSEQUENCES?

THIS IS TREASON AGAINST THE HEAVENS.
I HAVE TO STOP HER... OR SHE'LL END UP LIKE EBISU-SAMA'S PREDECES-SOR.
CRUNCH
KURA...
!
I THOUGHT I HEARD THE BELL... I COME TO CHECK, AND LOOK WHAT I FIND.
WHAT ARE YOU DOING HERE?! KAZUMA!

NO! IT'S HEAVENL GUARD ÔSHI!
BAH
PURGA-TORY!!!
CRACKLE
WAIT! THIS IS...
VNN
PUT YOUR PHALANGES AWAY! THAT BOX CONTAINED A TRAITOR WHO REBELLED AGAINST HER EXCELLENCY!!
WHAT IDEAS HAVE YOU PUT INTO YOUR MASTER'S HEAD?!

SEND UP THE BEA-CON!
BAH
HIGH TREA-SON!
FIP
FIP
HIGH TREA-SON!
BISHA-MONTEN HAS COMMIT-TED HIGH TREA-SON!!
NO!! VEENA WOULD NEVER...
STOP!
...
STOP, PLEASE!!

CHAPTER 61: RENEGADE

BISHAMON HAS COMMITTED HIGH TREASON!!
BISHAMON IS A TRAITOR!!
RRRAAAHH
HAD THEY ATTACHED A BELL TO SHIKKI?
RRAAH
BISHAMON IS A TRAITOR!!
ALL OF YOU, HOLD!
THE CRAFTER STANDS BEFORE...

FWOOSH
?!
HE RAN AWAY.
WHAT?!
I THINK I UNDER-STAND HOW HE FEELS...
I WOULDN'T BE SURPRISED IF THE HEAVENS TOOK SOMEONE HE LOVED, LIKE IT DIDN'T EVEN MATTER.
OTHERWISE HE WOULD NEVER CAL YOU "THE LIKES OF A GOD."
NOW I'M GLAD I HAVE THIS NAME...
BECAUSE I CAN FIGHT THEM!!

BAH
SHIKKI, STOP!
WE MUSTN'T BE THE FIRST TO STRIKE ...
HERE IT COMES.
BZZZ
WHAT IS THAT SOUND?
BZZ
BZZZZ
BAM

BZZZZZZZ
INSECT ?!
GWAAAAAAAAH!
AAAAAAH! AAAAAAH!!
I WILL DEVOUR YOU!!

BASH
A LOCUST?
THE EMPEROR OF INSECTS.
HMPH.
YOUR SCHEME IS QUITE TRANS-PARENT, BISHAMON!
KIUN!
BAH

FLASH
GIVE HER SPORT!
RUMBLE RUMBLE
CLENCH...
RUMBLE
THAT IS WHY...
I KNEW ONCE SHIKKI WAS FREED, THIS WOULD FOLLOW...
...I'D HOPED TO DEFEAT HIM FIRST!

FLASH
DO NOT ...

...BAR MY WAY!
RATTLE
RATTLE
RATTLE
AAAAAAHHH
WHAM
DID IT HIT US?!
I FELT A ZAP!
RUMBLE
RUMBLE
THE SKY WAS CLEAR A FEW MINUTES AGO...
RUMBLE

CRACKLE
CLANG
DOW
BISHAMON-SAN IS FIGHTING AGAINST THE HEAVENS.
KA-CLANG
WHY? AND WHERE'S FUJISAKI-SEMPAI?!
YATO!
IS YATO HERE, TOO?!
BISHAA? A REBEL?!

SHE WOULD NEVER DO THAT AND YOU KNOW IT.
IMMA GO JOIN BISHAA, TOO!!
YOU STAY OUT OF THIS! YOU'LL ONLY MAKE EVERYTHING WORSE.
WHAT WERE YOU THINKING, BISHAMON-SAN? WHAT-EVER YOUR REASONS MAY HAVE BEEN... YOU KNOW THEY'LL NEVER LET A REBEL GO FREE.
URP BLERR
THIS IS NOTHING COMPARED TO WHAT HAPPENED WITH EBISU-DONO!
BISHAMONTEN-DONO COMMANDS KAZUMA! I DON'T WANT TO GO ANYWHERE NEAR THAT.
NO, I HEARD THEY HAVE KAZUMA IN CUSTODY...
DO YOU THINK HE INCITED THIS?
TOSS
AN UN-FAITHFUL BLESSED VESSEL...
I DO ENVY HER HER BLESSED VESSEL, BUT SHE CERTAINLY SEEMS TO ATTRACT TROUBLE.
EXCUSE ME, ÔSHI. YOU KNOW I'VE INVESTED A LOT IN THESE DIVINE COUNCILS.
I WOULD LIKE TO EXERCISE MY POWER OF VETO AGAINST THIS SUB-JUGATION ORDER.

THEN LET'S PUT IT TO A VOTE. MOST OF THE GODS HAVE STAYED HERE.
THAT IS BECAUSE EVERY GOD WITH ANY PRIDE IN HIS POWERS HAS JOINED THE SUBJUGATION FORCE.
WHAT ABOUT YOU, EBISU-SAMA? WOULD YOU LIKE TO TRY YOUR SKILL?
YOU HAVE NO SUCH POWER.
THAT'S ENOUGH!
I FOUND HIM!
IS SUBJUGATION REALLY THE ONLY SOLUTION YOU CAN THINK OF?!
THE HEAVENS ARE ALWAYS RIGHT.
THAT MEANS *YOU* ARE RIGHT AS WELL, EBISU-SAMA.

IF YOU THINK HER EXCELLENCY IS WRONG, PERHAPS YOU SHOULD USE YOUR OWN POWER TO SHOW HER.
THEN...
THEN I WILL ...
I WILL ISSUE A DIVINE DECREE TO MAKE WAR AND VIOLENCE POWER-LESS...
WAKA !!

AND INSTATE MONEY AS THE DRIVING POWER BEHIND EVERY-THING IN THIS WORL—

HOW COULD YOU SUGGEST SUCH A THING! YOU KNOW THAT'S NOT ACCEPTABLE!!

BUT HE'S SO CUTE..
I-I CAN'T BELIEVE I'M HEARING THIS FROM EBESSAMA.
IN-DEED ...
IT IS UNUSUAL TO SEE EBISU-SAN IN SUCH A RAGE.
BUT EVERY GOD HAS THAT ASPECT TO HIM.
BECAUSE WE ARE VERY TRUE TO THE PRAYERS WITH WHICH WE HAVE BEEN ENTRUSTED.
IN THE SAME VEIN...
WHETHER THEY KNOW IT OR NOT, EVERYONE HERE IS ABANDONING BISHAMON-SAN. THAT GOES FOR KUNIMI...
...AND FOR YOU, DAIKOKU-KUN, OR YOU WOULD NOT BE STANDING HERE DOING NOTHING.
BLEGH, URGH...
...!
WELL, I KNOW HOW YOU FEEL.
I WAS HUMAN ONCE, MYSELF.

AND WHEN A HUMAN HAS SOMEONE H WANTS TO PROTECT...
...HE IS VERY TRUE TO THAT... AND VERY CRUEL.

SO THEY SAID *WHY* THEY WERE CANCELING THE REST OF THE COUNCIL.
ZOOM
BUT I WAS SO FAR AWAY I COULDN'T HEAR IT.

WHAT'S THIS ABOUT HIGH TREASON?

THE WORST OF THE EIGHT UNPARDON-ABLE CRIMES. IN THE HEAVENS, THAT MEANS A-REBELLIN' AGAINST HER EXCELLENCY.

SO BASICALLY IT'S A COUP D'ÉTAT?
-YEP.

RUSTLE
ANYHOW, PUT THAT THERE CLOTH OVER YER HEAD.
SO AS YOU DON'T CATCH NO FUTURE TROUBLE IF ANYTHING SHOULD HAPPEN.
OH, IS THAT WHAT THESE ARE FOR...
SO WE'R ON THE HEAVENS EXECUTIC SQUAD TOO...
IT'S JUST LIKE WHAT HAPPENED TO EBISU-SAMA.
I DIDN'T THINK WE'D EVER BE ON THIS SIDE OF IT.

STRA—?!
YUKINÉ, HELP ME.
SHA- N HAS OME KILL THER.
SHE'S THE ONE—THE TRAITOR THE HEAVENS ARE GOING AFTER. SHE WANTED TO KILL FATHER SO BADLY THAT SHE COMMITTED HIGH TREASON TO GET THE BURIAL VESSEL.
HE MANAGED TO GET AWAY FROM HER, BUT I'M STILL WORRIED.
I'M GOING DOWN TO HELP HIM.
BUT I DON'T KNOW IF I CAN DO IT ALL ON MY OWN...

IF YOU WANT TO PROTECT YATO...
...YOU'LL LET THE HEAVENS PUNISH BISHAMON.

YATO!
YATO, HOLD ON A MINUTE!
DO WE REALLY HAVE TO GO?
WHAT, YOU'RE CHICK-ENING OUT?
Y-YEAH, BUT... THIS COULD BE DIF-FERENT.
WE STOP ALL THE TROUBLE BEFORE IT HAPPENS. ISN'T THAT HOW WE DO THINGS?
WE WON'T BE ANY HELP!

WE'RE GOING TO STOP A COL D'ÉTAT, AND YOU'RE A BLESSED VESSEL. HO WOULD YO NOT BE AN HELP?
YOU LOOK LIKE YOU KNOW SOME-THING...
WHAT'S GOING ON?
N-NOTHING.
CAN YOU SWEAR THAT TO ME?
...
...COM SEKK
HEY!
SWISH
WOO! STOM-ACH DROP!

KHEEN
N-NO, COME BACK!

GRK
THRUST
CLANG
WHACK
...ISN'T THAT BISHAMON?
WHOA ?!
HEY.
LIKE
WHA... WHAT IS SHE DOING?!

CLANNNG
NEARGH!
...SO THIS IS THE BURIAL VESSEL? BUT I'D HEARD THAT SHE COULD TEAR HEAVEN AND EARTH ASUNDER.
TMP
THAT MAY HAVE BEEN TRUE BEFORE SHE WAS SEALED AWAY...BUT IT WOULD APPEAR THAT SHE IS NOT BLESSED FOR BISHAMONTEN-SAMA.
CRACKLE CRACKLE

IF THIS IS THE EXTENT OF HER POWER I DON'T THINK WE'LL NEED ANY HELP TO QUIET HER.
PSST...
WHAT... SHE'S NOT EVEN AS MIGHTY AS CHÔKI...
...
CHING
THEN LET US TAKE HER HEAD FORTHWITH. ...KIUN, WE'LL MAKE SHORT WORK OF THIS.
MIND YOU DON'T HARM THE THINGS OF THE NEAR SHORE.
YES, MY LORD...
PLEASE BE CAREFUL, KIUN.
YES.

I WILL.
FLASH
!
ゴゴ...
ROLLLL
RUMBLE
ゴロゴロ...
RUMBLE
BOOoOM

UH...
RATTLE
RATTLE
RATTLE
OHO...

IF ANY IS WORTHY OF A NAME THAT WOULD SUNDER HEAVEN AND EARTH, IT IS KIUN...

GNN
BUT IT CANNOT BE HELPED.
RUMBLE
RUMBLE
RUMBLE
BEEEEEEP!!
H-HONK
MURMUR
MURMUR
MURMUR
I HAD A MIND TO LET YOU SPORT MORE FREELY, BUT IT IS NOT TO BE.
YOU CANNOT MAKE A NAME FOR YOURSELF IN THIS PEACEFUL WORLD UNLESS YOU BECOME BLESSED.
IT IS TRULY A SHAME ...

SHIK-
KI...
I HAVEN'T HAD MY FILL!
...NOT YET.
AFTER ALL THE HAVOC SHE'S ALREADY WROUGHT...
...SHIKKI YET HAS NO INTENTION OF STAYING HER HAND.
ZSHHH

THUNK
THUNK
THUNK
SHOONK

SLASH
WHACK

OW...?!
WHAT ARE YOU DOING?
ETTING YOUR OOBS FLY ROUND LIKE THAT.

YAT —?
SHH!
ZSH
THEY'RE WATCHING. KEEP PRETENDING WE'RE FIGHTING.

I THOUGHT YOU WERE LOOKING FOR MY DAD. WHAT'S WITH THE COUP D'ÉTAT?
WHACK
CLANG
I FOUND HIM, BUT HE FLED.
AND THIS ENSUED.
WHA?!
KA-CLANG

I GET THAT YO DIDN'T WANT TO BRING ALL YOU GUYS INTO THIS...
BUT BOY ARE YOU LOST WITHOUT KAZUMA.
INDEED... YOU SPEAK TRULY.

!
YOU KNOW, WHEN YOU LOOK AT ME LIKE THAT...
THOONK
IF... IF YOU HADN'T MADE MENTION OF MY FAMILY...!
BAH

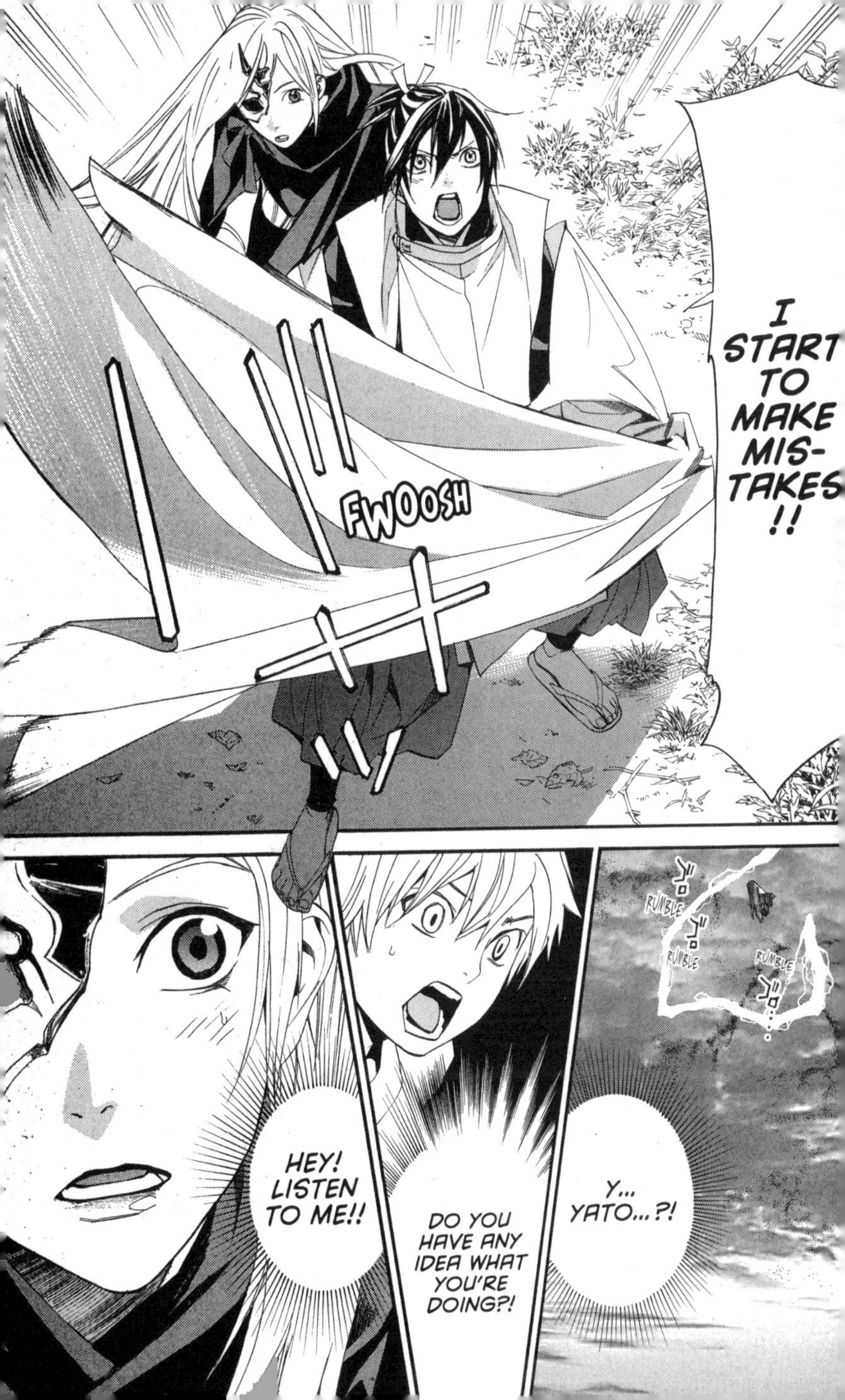
I START TO MAKE MIS-TAKES!!
FWOOSH
RUMBLE
RUMBLE
RUMBLE
Y... YATO...?!
DO YOU HAVE ANY IDEA WHAT YOU'RE DOING?!
HEY! LISTEN TO ME!!

KIUN!
BAH
LET SOMEONE ELSE TAKE BISHAMON'S HEAD.
YOUR OPPO-NENT...
...IS YATO-GAMI...
...AND HIS BLESSED ONE.
HAPTER 61 / END

見

神

SURE IS MIGHTY DULL BEIN' STUCK IN THE BACK-REARGUARD.
WONDER HOW THEY'RE GETTIN' ON IN THAT THERE SCUFFLE.
!
WHA HAP PEN ?!
BETRAYAL! SOMEONE SWITCHED OVER TO THE REBEL'S SIDE!
WHAT?!
OHO! WELL IF THAT DON'T BEAT ALL...
?!

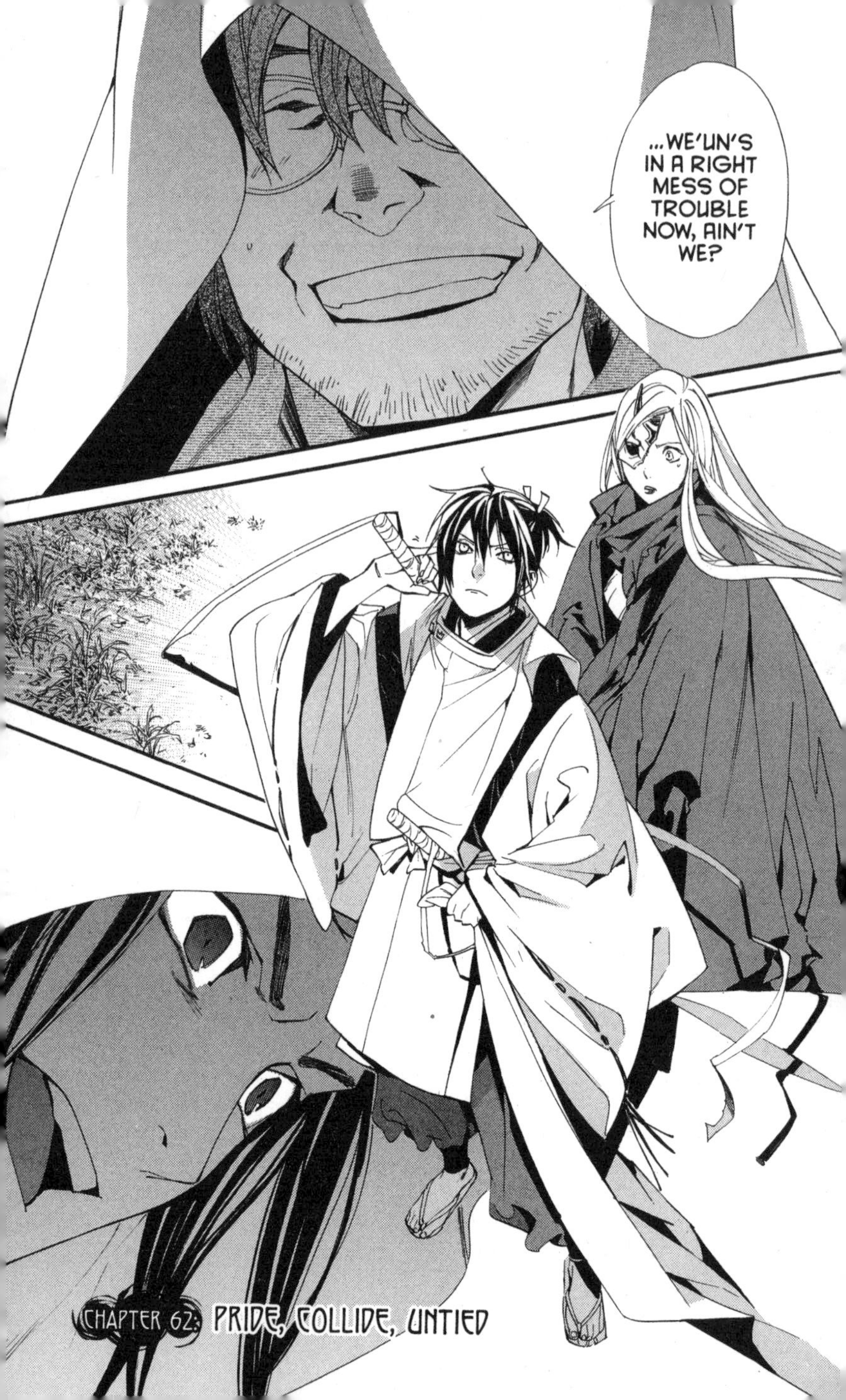
...WE'UN'S IN A RIGHT MESS OF TROUBLE NOW, AIN'T WE?
CHAPTER 62: PRIDE, COLLIDE, UNTIED

RUMBLE
RUMBLE
ROLL
ROLL
YATO, STAND DOWN... THEY'LL MARK YOU A TRAITOR, AS WELL!

...WAIT, YOU'RE O OUR SIDE I'M SO CONFUSE

DON'T BE STUPID! YOU'RE GOING UP AGAINST THE HEAVENS!

AND IT'S NOT JUST THAT, EITHER! BISHAMON-SAMA WANTS TO KILL YOUR FATHER.
AND YOU'RE GOING TO PROTECT HER?
YOU'RE CUTTING YOUR OWN LIFELINE!
...SO YOU'RE SAYING BISHAMON COULD BE A PROBLEM, AND I SHOULD LET THE HEAVENS NIP IT IN THE BUD?
SOUNDS LIKE SOME-THING THE STRAY WOULD COME UP WITH.
B-DMP

THANKS FOR WORRYING ABOUT ME, YUKINÉ.
BUT I'M THROUGH WITH REGRETS!
HE SOWED THESE SEEDS.

SWISH
MAYBE I'LL DO WHAT HE SAYS AND TAKE SOME RESPONSIBILITY!

YAT ...
HMPH! DON'T FALL FOR ME!
HEH.
STAY YOUR CONCERN. THAT SHALL NEVER HAPPEN.
SIGH ...
NEVER?! WELL I'M NOT AIMING FOR A HAPPY ENDING WITH YOU, EITHER!!

YATO.
ENOUGH. LOOK AROUND.

FLASH

SHANG
A CHURL WHO KNOWS NO RIGHTEOUS-NESS HAS JOINED THE CRIMINAL'S RANKS!
I WILL STRIKE DOWN THE WORTHLESS LOUT!
NO ONE LAG BEHIND NOW!
ONWARD!
YATO! KEEP YOUR WITS ABOUT YOU!
YOU KNOW THEY CAN'T BEAT ME.
ZSHH

GLINT
I HAVE A BLESSED VESSEL!
YOU SHOW FINE METTLE.
BUT PRIDE AND CONCEIT ARE NOT THE SAME THING.
SWOOSH
TAKEMIKA-ZUCHI IS A WARRIOR GOD, AND HIS SHINKI ARE ALL SOLDIERS! SO...
YEAH, I GET IT. HE'S A BATTLE FREAK!
THUMP
THUMP
THUMP
THUMP

BOOM
WELL, WELL, YOU LOOK HAPPY TO SEE ME!

RATTLE
RATTLE
RATTLE
OH, COME *ON,* YABOKU.
WHAT IS THAT IDIOT SON OF MINE DOING?
HERE I WAS TRYING TO KEEP HIM OUT OF SIGHT.
HONESTLY, HE ALWAYS HAS TO BE IN THE SPOTLIGHT...
COME, CHIKI.
PASH

ARE YOU WORRIED ABOUT YATO, FATHER?
WHY WOULDN'T I BE? YOU KNOW AS WELL AS I DO...
...THAT HE CAN'T REINCAR-NATE.
YOU THINK YATO WILL LOSE.
...SO YOU'RE TAKING YUKINÉ'S SIDE, THEN?
HA HA HA. AWW, YOU'RE SO CUTE WITH THAT POUTY FACE, MIZUCHI.
YUKINÉ IS A GOOD RIVAL FOR YOU.

COME ON, IF I KNOW YOU, YOU'LL CATCH UP TO HIM IN NO TIME.
RUMBLE RUMBLE
...NOW THEN. HOW TO COLLECT YABOKU?
I DO EXPECT YUKINÉ...
...TO KEEP HIM IN ONE PIECE, BUT...
HIYAAAA!

WHACK

...HIYORI-CHAN.
WHAT DID YOU DO?!
WHY WOULD YOU MAKE THE HEAVENS ATTACK BISHAMON-SAN LIKE THAT?!
I KNOW YOU'RE BEHIND THIS, SEMPAI!
IT'S NOT WHAT YOU THINK. SHE WAS BEING BAD WITHOUT MY HELP.

I WARNED HER...BUT SHE DOES HAVE THAT TEMPER.
TSU-GUHA, WAS IT?
THE POOR GIRL DIED FOR NOTHING.
I THOUGHT...
...I WARNED YOU, TOO, HIYORI-CHAN.

THMP
CLANK
THAK
HEY! WERE YOU EVEN LISTENING TO ME?!
WHAT?!
THIS IS WHERE THE GIRL IS SUPPOSED TO TREMBLE IN FEAR!
AND I SAW!
ZSH

YOU'R NOT GOING TO BEAT ME.
NOT ANY-MORE.
I WON'T LET YOU LAY A FINGER ON MY FAMILY!

SOME-HOW...
IT JUST DOESN'T SINK IN WITH THIS GIRL.

HM?
THIS ISN'T ANY FUN...
HERE!
FWAAAM!!
CLAMP
?!
CZHRUK
CLAMP
CLAMP
OOAAAARGH?!

DO YOU ADMIT DEFEAT?!
U-UNCLE... UNCLE!
GSH
THEN MAKE THE HEAVENS LEAVE! NOW! HELP BISHAMON-SAN!!
BRAG ABOUT THIS TO YABOKU. HE'LL CRY. LOL
YOU KNOW I CAN'T DO THAT.
CALM DOWN, MIZU-CHI.
THE HEAVENS DON'T RESPOND T PRODDING VERY WEL THEY WON MOVE UNLE IT'S FOR SOME GRE RIGHTEOU CAUSE.
A LITTLE RUMOR LIKE "BISHAMON TRANSGRESSED THE GODS' SECRET" DIDN'T BUDGE THEM AN INCH.
...BUT WOW! CAN YOU BELIEVE SHE RESORTED TO HIGH TREASON? ALL ON HER OWN, TOO!

YOU WANT ME TO HELP BISHAMON ?!
YOU'VE GOT IT WRONG. IT'S YABOKU WHO NEEDS HELP.
THAT IDIOT CAME OUT HERE TO HELP WITH THE SUBJU-GATION...
...BUT THEN HE TOOK PITY ON POOR WITTLE BISHAMON.
AND NOW HE'S GOT A GIANT TARGET ON HIS BACK.
WHAT ?!
AND HE'S UP AGAINST TAKEMIKAZUCHI, OF ALL PEOPLE.
ROLLLL
RUMBLE
RUMBLE

YOU KNOW WHAT HAPPENS TO A GOD...
...WHEN THE HEAVENS EXECUTE HIM, DON'T YOU, HIYORI-CHAN?
THER NOTH LEF
FORGET BISHAMON. SHE CAN BE REPLACED.
BUT WOULD YOU SIT BACK AND LET YABOKU DIE?

FLASH
PLEASE, HIYORI-CHAN.
I WANT TO HELP YABOKU.
POW
POW
POW
POW
POW

CRACKLE CRACKLE
RATTLE
RATTLE
RATTLE
OW...
GUESS IT'S NOT GONNA BE THAT EASY TO PARRY THE THUNDER BLADE!
THE LIGHTNING IS JUST A DISTRAC-TION!
SMART BOY, YUKINÉ.
THE REAL PAIN IN THE NECK IS THE GUY HIDING IN THE LIGHTNING.
FLASH

WHAM
GH
GH
TAKE-MIKA-ZUCHI!
GH

GRNGH
YOU SURPRISE ME...
SHARPER THAN THE THUNDER BLADE... WEIGHTIER THAN THE BURIER.
A BLESSED VESSEL TRULY IS A MARVEL!
SHING

WHACK
BUT HE PALES IN COMPARISON TO CHÔKI.
GH
GH
IT PAINS ME TO SEE A BLESSED VESSEL IN SUCH POOR SHAPE.
ALL FOR BEING IN THE SERVICE OF A MISCREANT GOD...

ZSH
KA-CLING
SHRR
WHACK
?!
GSH
PASH

SLASH

TMP...
HOW DARE HE...
THE NOV-ICE!!
EVEN OUR ENEMIES DESERVE OUR RESPECT.
WAI
BAH
CALM YOUR-SELVES.
KAUN, MIUN, SAIUN.
SH
SH
SH
IN LOOKING DOWN ON YOUR OPPONENT, YOU SCORN YOURSELF.

WE ARE VESSELS WITH NO TITLE,
WHICH IS EXACTLY WHY WE KNOW THE PRIDE THAT IS FOUND IN OUR OWN NAMES!
A RARE SIGHT...
NOW...
HAVE AT YOU!!
SMIRK
にはあ
A FIRE HAS BEEN LIT IN KIUN!

BRING IT ON!!
FLASH
CLUNK

CREAK
WHO'S THERE?
...THE HEAVENLY GUARD? WELL, IT DOESN'T MATTER.
ARE YOU HERE TO MAKE ME SING?

I'M SORRY, BUT YOUR SPELLS WON'T WORK ON ME.
SO I DON'T KNOW HOW I CAN PROVE IT TO YOU.
BUT BISHAMON-SAMA WOULD NEVER REBEL AGAINST...
WH... WHAT IS IT?
KAZU-MA.
RÔRÔ. [ARTICU-LATE.]

I TOLD YOU, YOUR SPELLS ...
!!
YANK
SHOONK...
DID YOU INCITE YOUR MASTER TO REBEL-LION?
NO!
?!

IMPOSSIBLE...
THEN BISHAMONTEN-SAMA IS ACTING ON HER OWN?
Y-YES.
DRIP
DRIP
AND YOU KNEW NOTHING...? NOR DID ANY OF THE HA CLAN?
SHE'S MAKING ME SING.
BUT SHE'S JUST AN ORDINARY SHINKI.
IF I HAD KNOWN, I WOULD HAVE STOPPED HER!
I...
THEN SHE PLOTTED THIS INSURRECTION WITHOUT ANY HELP?
...CAN'T EVEN RAISE MY HEAD...
IT'S NOT AN INSURRECTION!!

VEENA ONLY WANTS TO DESTROY THE CRAFTER!!
SHE'S TOO HIGH ABOVE ME.

BUT I'M A BLESSED VESSEL.

I WAS SO PROUD OF THAT!

THUD
SHHHHHH
POW
POW
POW

ROLLLLL
RUMBLE
RUMBLE
RUMBLE
CHAPTER 62 / END

劉

邑

神

OH... EBISU.
WHAT'S UP? DO YOU NEED SOME-THING?

WHAT...?

CHAPTER 63: ECSTASY

YUKI...
KHING
YATO!!
ARE YOU OKAY?! HE GOT YOU REALLY BAD...
THEY JUST GOT SO POWERFUL ALL OF A SUDDEN! ...I KNOW THAT'S JUST AN EXCUSE...
I'M SORRY I LET YOU GET HURT!!
I'M PREPARED FOR SOME CUTS AND SCRAPES. YOU'RE NOT ARMOR, AFTER ALL.
PULL THE STRING FROM MY SLEEVE AND PUT IT AROUND MY NECK.
STRING?
DON'T... WORRY ABOUT IT.
TAKEMIKAZUCHI WAS JUST TOO FAST FOR ME TO BLOCK. ...AND THE SKANK *JUST* TOLD ME NOT TO LET MY GUARD DOWN. DAMMIT.
OWW.

WHERE *IS* BISHA-MON?!
RUMBLE
RUMBLE
POW
POW

HA.
OF COURSE ...
BUT SHE NEEDS HELP.
SEKKI.
Y-YOU CAN'T FIGHT IN THAT CONDITION!
I'LL BE FINE. I CAN STILL MOVE.

NO, PUT IT UNDER MY ARM FIRST... OWWW!
!
HOW AM I SUPPOSED TO KNOW?!
HIYORI?!
WH-WHAT ARE YOU DOING OUT HERE?
WE'RE KIND OF UNDER ATTACK RIGHT NOW...
PRESS

FUJISAKI-SEMPAI TOLD ME...
...THAT BISHAMON-SAN IS WANTED BY THE HEAVENS FOR HIGH TREASON.
BUT HE ALSO SAID TO FORGET ABOUT HER,
BECAUSE YABOKU IS THE ONE THAT NEEDS SAVING.
I... COULDN'T ARGUE WITH THAT...

THE OLD MAN IS MEDDLING AGAIN...
OH, HE DENIED THAT.
HMPH. LIKE WE CAN TRUST HIM.
YATO ...
IS THERE ANYTHING WE CAN DO TO HELP HER?
I DON'T WANT TO LET YOU *OR* BISHAMON-SAN DIE.
I KNOW IT'S NOT THAT SIMPLE!
BUT...
...THAT'S NO REASON TO DO NOTHING. THAT WOULD BE LIKE ABANDONING HER.

...DAD ALWAYS DOES THAT. HE THINKS HE CAN CONTROL PEOPLE AND GODS LIKE HE DOES AYAKASHI.
I'M DONE LETTING HIM HAVE HIS WAY!
BESIDES, BISHAMON'S A DRINKING BUDDY OF MINE! I WAS NEVER GOING TO ABANDON HER!
DON'T YOU WORRY! I HEARD YOUR PRAYER, HIYORI! LOUD AND CLEAR!
!
...NO.

I DON'T AGREE.
ROLL ゴゴ…
RUMBLE ゴロ
ゴロ RUMBLE
NOW, WHERE OH WHERE IS YATOGAMI HIDING?
SURELY HE HASN'T WITHDRAWN INTO RETIRE-MENT.

I THOUGHT HIS DEMISE IMMINENT...
BUT HE STRUCK BACK.
NOT BAD FOR A MISCREANT GOD!

I-I'M SO TER-RIBLY SORRY FOR ALLOWING YOU TO BE INJURED...
IT IS OF NO CONSEQUENCE. NOTHING HAS EVER CUT THROUGH SAIKI BEFORE.
AND YOU HAVE DONE WELL TO WITHSTAND THE BLOWS OF A BLESSED VESSEL.
YOU HAVE MY THANKS, SAIUN!

THAT KNAVE. HE MADE NO MOVE TO BLOCK THE SWORD CUTTING INTO HIS OWN FLESH, BUT TOOK A SWING AT ME INSTEAD.
HE'S A FEISTY ONE, THIS RAGING SPIRIT!

MAGNIFICENT! THE TALE OF THIS SUBJUGATION WILL BE A NEW MYTH!
KIUN!
THIS IS THE THREAT I DESIRED!!

...INDEE
BUT DON'T LET YOUR ENJOYMENT OF THE BATTLE TURN TO YOUR DETRIMENT.
YOU HAVE BEEN WORSHIPED FOR MANY AGES. DON'T BE CARELESS WITH THE LIFE THAT'S BEEN GIVEN YOU.

HMPH
A NEW MYTH?
IN WHOSE MYTHOLOGY?
AND YOU.
YOU KNEW THAT YATOGAMI WOULDN'T RELENT, AND YET YOU, TOO, REFUSED TO BLOCK. YOU FOLLOWED THROUGH ON YOUR SWING.
WITH NO THOUGHT FOR YOURSELF... OR YOUR SHINKI.

THIS MAN IS PLAYING WITH FIRE.

AS YOUR GUIDE, I CAN'T LET YOU RUN OFF INTO DANGER.
...EVEN IF YOU ARE ANSWERING A PRAYER FROM HIYORI!

I'M TELLING YOU... YOU'RE TALKING LIKE THE STRAY.
OKAY, SO WHAT ABOUT DAIKOKU-SAN? OR KUNIMI-SAN? NONE OF THEM ARE COMING TO HELP.
BECAUSE THEY'RE SCARED! THEY KNOW WHAT HAPPENS WHEN YOU OPPOSE THE HEAVENS!
I DON'T THINK HIYORI IS ASKING FOR ANYTHING WRONG.
BUT IT'S *MY* JOB TO KEEP YOU SAFE, YATO.
I CAN'T LET YOU GO OUT THERE TO BE HUNTED DOWN LIKE AN ANIMAL!
THE HEAVENS DON'T KNOW WHY WE'RE OUT HERE!
SO LET'S AT LEAST GET AWAY FROM THE FIGHTING!
WE CAN UST GET OUT OF HERE, HEY'LL...

...Y—
YUKINÉ, THAT'S IT!
WHY DIDN'T I SEE IT BEFORE?!
THEY *DON'T* KNOW WHY WE'RE OUT HERE!
SO WE JUST HAVE TO TELL THEM!
T-TELL THEM?
LISTEN. THE EXECUTION SQUAD IS JUST A HASTY MISHMASH OF FIGHT-ERS.
IT'S A RANDOM GROUP OF VOLUN-TEERS!

BUT THERE ARE MILLIONS OF GODS, AND SOME OF THEM ARE LIKE EBISU. THEY DON'T LIKE TO GO AROUND KILLING EVERYTHING.
THIS UBJUGATION RDER WASN'T UNANIMOUS DECISION!
SO IF WE JUST GO OUT THERE AND EXPLAIN THAT THIS ISN'T HIGH TREASON,
MAYBE WE CAN GET THE HEAVENS TO CHANGE THEIR MIND! RIGHT?!
YOU KNOW THAT'S NOT GONNA WORK!!
I WILL FIGHT THE HEAVENS OVER THIS!!

...!

TAKEMIKAZUCHI I'LL GRAB THE ARROGAN BULLY BY THE SCRUFF OF HIS NECK AND DEMAND THAT THEY LISTEN TO US!
YUKI-NÉ!!
I KNEW IT.
...THAT'S WHY SEKKI WAS KIND OF DULL TODAY. YOU DON'T WANT TO GET ON THE HEAVENS' BAD SIDE.
RÓLLLL
RATTLE
RATTLE
?!
I CAN'T LET YOU FIGHT THE HEAVENS!

YOU WANT TO BURY THE HATCHET TO KEEP ME FROM BEING BRANDED A TRAITOR? ...THAT'S A GOOD DECISION.
RUMBLE
RUMBLE
KA-CRACK
BUT WE'RE PAST THAT NOW.
STUPID TAKÉ— HE'S LIKE A WHOLE OTHER PER-SON SINCE HE GOT HERE.
THAT KIUN... HE'S A GOOD INSTRUMENT.
YOU HAVE MY PERMIS-SION.
I CAN'T FIGHT IF SEKKI'S GONNA GO BAMBOO SWORD ON ME.

BOOM
SEKKI !!
RATTLE
RATTLE
Y-YATO ...
CRACKLE
CRACKLE
RATTLE
RATTLE
BRING TAKE-MIKA-ZUCHI DOWN !!
DON'T YOU WORRY ABOUT ME, HIYORI! I'M A GOD OF HAPPINESS! ☆
I'LL RESOLVE THIS PEACE-FULLY!
OW.
PSHH
...!

...FINISHED WITH YOUR LITTLE CHAT? YATOGAMI.
SWISH
NO, I WAS JUST GETTING READY TO *START* A CHAT. WITH YOU.
PASH
HA HA HA, YOU WISH TO TALK?!
TH-THIS IS PEACE-FUL?
THEN...
LET'S HEAR YOUR PIECE!

I CAN'T LET...
MY LORD
YATO
...DIE IN THIS POINTLESS BATTLE.

BISHA-MONTEN...
IMPOSTOR WHO FALSELY TAKES THE HEAVENS' NAME UPON YOU!
BASH
!
HUFF...
HUFF
NEXT!
HUFF
HEY, HAT'S RONG?

"THE LIKES OF A GOD," EH?
I AM BEGINNING TO FEEL HE MAY BE RIGHT.
WHICH OF US IS BEING USED?

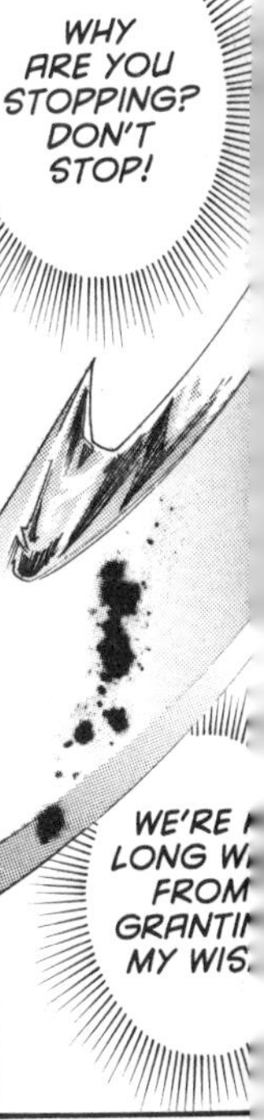
WHY ARE YOU STOPPING? DON'T STOP!
WE'RE LONG W FROM GRANTI MY WIS

...

...HAVE YOU NOT HAD YOUR FILL, SHIKKI!
HAVE YOU NOT TAKEN ENOUGH HEAVENLY HEADS?!

...NOT YET.

I WANT THE HEAD...
...OF THE ONE ABOVE THOSE CLOUDS, THE WHO LOOKS DOWN ON US FROM WAY UP ON THAT PEDESTAL!
GO!!
GRNK
!
ザァ
ZSHHHHHH

SAKUYA-BIMÉ...
?
KRIK
FLUTTER FLUTTER
HRGH?!
GSH

KAGU-
TSUCHI
...!
FWOOOOM
GYAAA-
AARGH!

WHOOOOSH
WHOOSH
NOW!
FIRE!
SHINATSUHIKO!
SWOOSH

THUNK
THUNK
THUNK
BWOH
BWOH
BWOH
OOHH!!
KEEP YOUR WITS ABOUT YOU! WE ARE AGAINST BISHAMON!
YATAGARASU!!

HER LOCUSTS HAD THEIR TURN!
NOW *YOU* WILL DEVOUR *HER!!*
BAM
CAW CAW
CAW
CAW CAW

AAAH! WAAAH!!
STOP! STOP IT, YOU LITTLE—!!
PECK PECK
TEAR
RIP
TEAR
SHRED
...
...THEY ARE DOING NO WRONG.
IS THIS THE END?
IF I WERE ON THEIR SIDE, I WOULD DO THE SAME.

WATCH OUT FOR A MAN...
...WITH A MONK'S STAFF.

FWOOSH
SMAAAAASH
!!
...?!
THE RUST HAS DULLED YOU, BURIAL VESSEL!
IS THIS ALL YOU CAN DO?!

I SHALL BREAK THROUGH THE HEAVENS' NET!
SET YOUR SIGHTS ON THE MAN WITH THE MONK'S STAFF!!

...
DON'T...
...ORDER ME AROUND!!
ZSHHH

THAT'S BISHAMON FOR YOU. SHE JUST WILL NOT RETIRE.
SHE'S SHOWERED WITH ARROWS, AND BEATEN BLACK AND BLUE, BUT NOTHING STOPS HER.
...DOES SHE INTEND TO DIE?
THEN WE HAVE BUT TO GRANT HER WISH.
ALONG WITH THE DISHONOR OF HAVING OPPOSED THE HEAVENS...

HERE, LITTLE GIRL.
COME UP HERE TO ME.
ATTRACT EVERYONE'S ATTENTION. BE THEIR TARGET.

SO THAT ALL OF THE HEAVENS...
...LOOK AWAY FROM YABOKU.

SHINE BRIGHT UNTIL YOUR BODY EVAPORATES.

AND CREATE A SHADOW WHERE WE CAN HIDE.

NORAGAMI / TO BE CONTINUED

神

COSTUME

HEY, YUKINÉ... I JUST NOTICED SOME-THING.
WHY DON'T YOU EVER DRESS LIKE ME?
...WHAT?
DANGLE...

WELL, ALL THE SKANK'S SHINKI AND ALL OF EBISU'S SHINKI WEAR MATCHING CLOTHES.
BOO-YA.
EVEN TAKÉ AND ALL HIS SHINKI HAVE THE SAME HAIR.
WHEN YOU GROW UP, YOU'LL WEAR A NECKTIE, OKAY?
VEENA DRESSES TO MATCH US.

SO WHY DON'T YOU COPY ME?
I WOULDN'T MIND.
UHH ...?
LET YUKINÉ-KUN WEAR WHAT HE WANTS. HE DOES WORK TO BUY HIS OWN CLOTHES.

BUT HOW AM I SUPPOSED TO FEEL YOU GUYS' LOVE THAT WAY?!
"YOU... GUYS" ?!
INNOCENT VICTIM

ATROCIOUS MANGA

...SO CLOSE! THE ANSWER IS B.
AWW, DANGIT!

SMARTPHONE SABLÉ

PRAYER OF A BLESSED VESSEL

VEENA... GOT THE BURIAL VESSEL?

THEN SHE'S SURE TO USE IT.
WHAT ON EARTH KIND OF...

WHAT KIND OF INSTRU-MENT WILL SHE BE?!!

DEPENDI ON THE VISUAL.. YOU'LL PAY, BURIER
I'M GOING TO APOLOGIZE WHILE I CAN.

KIUN COULD USE SOME ODOR ELIMINATOR

KIUN! IF ANYONE CAN BECOME A BLESSED VESSEL, YOU CAN!
NEVER GIVE UP!

HAVE MORE PASSION! TELL YOURSELF "I CAN DO IT"!
AIM FOR THE ACE!!

AND WHEN YOU START TO GIVE UP, WHEN YOU THINK IT'S HOPELESS, THINK OF YOUR MASTER! THINK OF ALL THE PEOPLE WHO SUPPORT YOU!
YOU'RE ALMOST THERE!!

YOU CAN DO IT, KIUN! SHOW THEM THAT BLESSEDITOS COME IN FAB THREES!!
BOO-YA!!
MY LORD IS STARTING TO REEK OF SHÛZÔ.

※ SHÛZÔ: A JAPANESE WEATHER GOD WHO HAS MADE A NAME FOR HIMSELF IN RECENT YEARS. A LATTER-DAY SUN GOD.

BRIBERY

WHY CAN'T I HELP BISHAMON-SAN?!
BECAUSE YOU COULD GET HURT, WAKA!!

I'M ONLY GOING TO TAKE ADVANTAGE OF HER ENEMIES' WEAKNESS AND SLAP THEM IN THE FACE WITH A STACK OF BILLS! I THINK THAT'S A LOT MORE PEACEFUL THAN ALL THIS BLOODSHED.
WHERE DID YOU LEARN TO PLAY SO DIRTY?!!
IF YOU START TAKING THAT ATTITUDE, THEN THE WORLD OF MEN WILL FOLLOW YOUR EXAMPLE!
DO YOU WANT TO TURN THIS COUNTRY INTO ONE THAT EN-COURAGES BRIBERY?!
10000

BESIDES, IT'S HUBRIS TO THINK YOU CAN MOVE PEOPLE WITH MONEY.
NNNGH...

...EVEN IF I GIVE YOU TIME OFF?
FEELINGS
WAVER

THE FOOD CHAIN

...THAT CLOUD LOOKS LIKE A WHALE.

AAH?! AAAAH!!
AN ENEMY ATTACK?!

WE WERE ATTACKED BY A SWARM OF LOCUSTS!
LOCUSTS?!
YATOCCHAN! BRING ME ONE OF THEM THERE CLOTHS!
?
JOLT
BZZZ
STAMP STAMP STAMP STAMP STAMP
IF IT'S LOCUSTS, WE BEST CATCH US SOME! WE'LL BOIL 'EM UP IN SOME SOY AND EAT 'EM FOR DINNER!!!
BAFF BAFF BAFF
GYAAAAHH!!!
PSH PSH PSH

SOMETIMES, YOU NEED TO SAY IT OUT LOUD

STUN
SO WHAT?! YOU GUYS HATE ME?!
WH- WHERE DO YOU GET THAT?!
THEY DO THEIR THING, WE DO OURS. THAT'S ALL.

LIAR!! EVERYBODY KNOWS THAT IF YOU LIKE SOME-ONE, YOU'LL WEAR MATCHING CLOTHES!!!
RUSTLE
EVERY-BODY KNOWS THIS?!

O-OKAY, WHAT ABOUT KOFUKU-SAN AND DAIKOKU-SAN?! THEY'RE AS CLOSE AS YOU CAN GET, BUT THEY DON'T MATCH!
ROLL
YEAH! YOU TELL HIM!

DAIKOKU DOESN'T REALLY LOVE KOFUKU!!!
STOMP
STOMP STOMP
INNOCENT VICTIM
I NEVER COMPLAIN ABOUT WEARING YOUR UNIFORM, HIYORI!
THAT'S BECAUSE YOU'RE THE PICTURE PERFECT PERVERT!

IF YOU LOVE ME, THEN PROVE IT!
SHOW ME WITH YOUR ATTI-TUDE!!
WHIIINE

WAAAAH
I WANNA DRESS LIKE TRIP-LETS!!
WAAAAH
...

IF IT'LL GET ME OUT OF THE TRIPLET LOOK...

D-DON'T WORRY, YATO. I...UM... WELL...
WHAT AM I DOING?
I LO...
WHAT AM I DOING?
M-M-M-ME, TOO. I LOV...

AWWW, GUYS ♡
STOMP STOMP
RIP
EWW, I'M ALL WET! x2
I HEART THE MISSUS !!!
DAIKOKUUU ~♡

THANK YOU TO EVERYONE WHO READ THIS FAR!

TRANSLATION NOTES

Japanese is a tricky language for most Westerners, and translation is often more art than science. For your edification and reading pleasure, here are notes on some of the places where we could have gone in a different direction in our translation of the work, or where a Japanese cultural reference is used.

Multipurpose shinki, page 5

The name Bishamon gave to the Burier is Nana, which means "seven." Seven is a symbolic number in many cultures, so the translators did a bit of research to see if there was a particular symbolism behind the number seven that might apply here. There are, of course, the Seven Gods of Fortune, whose honor has been besmirched by the crafter. In Japanese, there is also a term, *nanatsu dôgu*, meaning "seven tools," which refers to a complete set of tools that may be necessary for certain things. In the case of a warrior, the seven tools would be armor, sword, short sword, bow, arrows, cloak, and helmet. Shikki equips Bishamon with only five of these things (counting the mask as a helmet), but she replaces the bow and arrows with another sort of long-distance attack.

You will pay, page 36

The phrase *yurusanai*, rendered here as "you will pay," is a common chastisement against someone who has done something wrong. More literally, it means something like, "I will not forgive you," but these translators prefer a looser translation, because it is their opinion that, most of the time, an evildoer doesn't really care about forgiveness. It can also mean, "I will not allow you [to do this and go unpunished]," hence "you'll pay." In response, Kôto wonders who exactly Bishamon is that she has any power to make him pay.

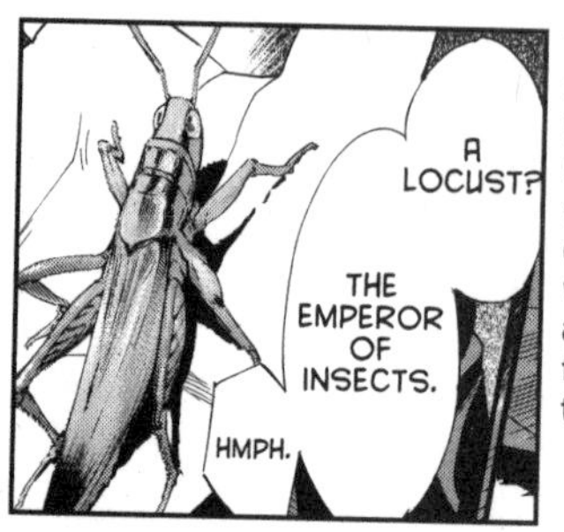

The emperor of insects, 56

More literally, Takemikazuchi describes the locust as the insect crowned with the title of emperor. This is a reference to the *kanji* character for locust, which is 蝗. What you see on the left side is the character for insect (虫), which can be found in the *kanji* for just about any insect name. On the right is the character for emperor (皇). And so, at least in writing, the locust is the emperor of insects.

I knew this would follow, page 57

Here Bishamon reveals another possible meaning behind the name Nana. The *kanji* character for Nana is 七, which originally meant "cut." The shape is something like a cross, with something trailing after it. As a pictograph, it represents *seppuku*, the ritual suicide. The cross represents the shape of the cuts made on the abdomen, and the tail is the blood and entrails that spill out after. By breaking the seal on this powerful shinki, Bishamon knows she is committing an act of treason, and in so doing, she is, in effect, committing suicide.

Eight Unpardonable Crimes, page 66

The Eight Unpardonable Crimes were the first eight crimes listed in the historical Japanese law system, the *Ritsuryô*, which was based on Chinese law and Confucianism. The worst of these crimes were against the emperor. In the Heavens, that means opposing the leader of the Heavens, Her Excellency.

Pride, Collide, Untied, page 90

The Japanese title of this chapter makes a beautiful play on words, where each word in the title builds on the one before it: *Hoko*, *Hokori*, *Hokorobi*, meaning "spear," "pride," and "open seams," respectively. The translators' efforts at maintaining this style of wordplay along with the meanings of the words met with failure, so they opted for rhyming words instead (and rearranged the order for rhythmic purposes). The "spear" in *hoko* can refer to any type of weapon, and is a homophone with the word for a shinki's phalanges, but it distinguishes itself from that term by using a different *kanji*, so it can refer to a shinki attack, but is not limited to one. The translators chose the word "collide" to indicate the collision of gods and shinki (weapons). *Hokorobi* is from the same word that the stray used in Volume Six when she was talking about bonds coming undone (see Chapter 21). It refers to an open seam, but often in the sense that the seam has burst or is otherwise falling apart.

A happy ending with you, page 93

What Yato originally said was that he would not raise a flag for her, but even though Yato would not be above such things, the English version may have more vulgar connotations than the Japanese. A "flag" is an action or event in a story that foreshadows future developments—in this case, a sign that he and Bishamon will end up in a romantic relationship. It refers to dating sims—video games in which the player has a choice of multiple characters that he or she can attempt to woo. If a choice in a game brings the player closer to a character, that choice "raises a flag." In other words, if Yato's life were a dating sim, he would do nothing to get Bishamon's ending.

Torii, page 111

The gates pictured behind Yato are called *torii*, and have appeared many times in this series before, but never in such great numbers. The *torii* is the symbol of a Shinto shrine, and represents the transition from the profane to the sacred—once someone walks through the *torii* onto the shrine grounds, they have entered sacred territory. The presence of so many *torii* indicates that this is a shrine to Inari, or Uka-no-Mitama, the god of agriculture who made an appearance in the previous volume. At least in the case of some Inari shrines, successful businesses will donate a *torii* as thanks to this god of industry, and the Fushimi Inari Shrine in Kyoto has ten thousand of them. The shrine where this battle is taking place is the Tokyo version of that shrine—the Higashi Fushimi Inari Shrine.

Playing with fire, page 147

The word Kiun used here to describe his master was *ayaui*, which has a variety of meanings, including "dangerous," "apt to fall into danger," and "unreliable." He is concerned that Takemikazuchi's lust for battle and eagerness to obtain a blessed vessel will put all of them in danger—in other words, Takemikazuchi is a danger to himself and all his shinki, which makes him an unreliable master.

I SHALL BREAK THROUGH THE HEAVENS' NET!
SET YOUR SIGHTS ON THE MAN WITH THE MONK'S STAFF!!

The Heavens' net, page 167

In Japanese, the *tenmô*, or "heavens' net," is a metaphor for something like karma. If someone does something wrong, they will eventually find themselves caught in the heavens' net, and then be forced to pay the consequences for what they've done. In this case, the net is somewhat more literal, and made of crows and other divine beings who will make Bishamon pay for her treason.

Smartphone Sablé, page 172

The city of Kamakura is famous for many things, including a cookie called *hato sablé*, where *sablé* is a French word for "shortbread cookie," and *hato* is a Japanese word meaning "dove" or "pigeon." Apparently Yato has made his own brand of pigeon shortbread cookies, named after his beloved Smartphone. It is also clear from the picture that the practice of repurposing cookie tins as storage for sewing supplies is universal.

Shûzô, page 173

Aim for the Ace! is the name of a sports manga from the '70s about a tennis player, which is relevant as Shûzô Matsuoka is a famous Japanese tennis player who has made many appearances on TV. There are rumors that he controls the weather, because he's so passionate that the heat of his emotion warms the surrounding area, and whenever he leaves the country, it gets colder. One of his more famous appearances was in a commercial for a certain famous odor eliminator, in which his face appears in the sky on a giant sun that freshens the entire nation of Japan with spray bottles full of the magic elixir.

As the reader may remember, the Japanese word for Blesseditos is "Hafuris." The U is almost silent, so the name sounds something like "haf-reez." It easily may have reminded Kiun of something that may eliminate the stench of passionate tennis players, but unfortunately for the translators, they could not come up with any word that might mean "blessed vessel" and also remind the readers of freshness. Therefore, they were forced to resort to the use of a terrible pun, and they would like to apologize. For the sake of this pun, the translators express a hope that Takemikazuchi would not count the Burier among the Blesseditos.

YOU CAN DO IT, KIUN! SHOW THEM THAT BLESSEDITOS COME IN FAB THREES!!
MY LORD IS STARTING TO REEK OF SHÛZÔ.
BOO-YA!!
※ SHÛZÔ: A JAPANESE WEATHER GOD WHO HAS MADE A NAME FOR HIMSELF IN RECENT YEARS. A LATTER-DAY SUN GOD.

Divine retainer, page 183

The word actually used here is *kenzokushin*, which refers to the messenger of a deity. This is usually an animal that appears to people and delivers messages for the god. However, since Tenjin's main symbol is the plum blossom, his *kenzokushin* would be a plum spirit instead of an animal. The first portion of the word, *kenzoku*, refers to "a member of one's family," and this being *Noragami*, the double meaning is likely very intended.

Surprise Character Trivia Part 2

Tenjin: He does fly into a rage occasionally, so he always has three shinki on hand to cast purgatory. His main criteria for adopting shinki is whether or not they can draw a borderline against their master.

Tsuyu: It is rare to instate a divine retainer as a guide.

Mayu: Feels uncomfortable around large fires.

Ebisu: He's very soft, as you would expect from a Leech Child.

Kunimi: His only job for around 200 years was tying Waka's shoelaces...

Adachitoka: Kunimi can't understand what's not to like about Waka.

Adachitoka

Noragami: Stray God volume 16 is a work of fiction. Names, characters, places, and incidents are the products of the author's imagination or are used fictitiously. Any resemblance to actual events, locales, or persons, living or dead, is entirely coincidental.

A Kodansha Comics Trade Paperback Original.

Published in the United States by Kodansha Comics, an imprint of Kodansha USA Publishing, LLC, New York.

Publication rights for this English edition arranged through Kodansha Ltd., Tokyo.

First published in Japan in 2016 by Kodansha Ltd., Tokyo.

ISBN 978-1-63236-257-5

Printed in the United States of America.

www.kodanshacomics.com

9 8 7 6 5 4 3 2 1

Translation: Alethea Nibley & Athena Nibley
Lettering: Lys Blakeslee
Editing: Lauren Scanlan
Kodansha Comics edition cover design: Phil Balsman